Where Is the Cat?

by Sam Baker

Glenview, Illinois • Boston, Massachusetts
Chandler, Arizona • Upper Saddle River, New Jersey

Where is the cat?
The cat is in the grass.

Where is the cat?
Look up!

Where is the cat?
There it is!

Where is the cat?
Silly cat!

Where is the cat?
I see it again.

Where is the cat?
The cat is in a bag.

The cat is with me!